My Dream of Freedom:

From Holocaust to My Beloved America

.

Helen Colin

.

As told to

Elizabeth Dettling Moreno

Kamy Schiffman

and Lynn Bliss

ACKNOWLEDGEMENTS

Special thanks to Elizabeth Dettling Moreno, Kamy Schiffman and Lynn Bliss for taking down my story. Thank you to Suzanne Sutherland, Mary Lee Webeck and photographer Kelly Webeck as well, for invaluable assistance. My sincere thanks, too, to Nadine Payn, Robert Arndt and Yardena Bobyk for their cherished and wholehearted support of this project. Cover layout credits go to Heidi Dorey. Finally, I want to express my deep appreciation to Pamela Fagan Hutchins who was the guardian angel who so lovingly guided this book to its ultimate publication.

CONTENTS

Section Three:

Life in the Camps

Section Four:

Life in America

Section Five

INTRODUCTION

This book was written for my family and friends, as well as the public, so that they will learn from my experiences. We must protect our future so that no one will ever endure and the world will never again see suffering like those who went through the Holocaust. It is my hope to bring this tragedy to all people and encourage vigilance against atrocities, to promote tolerance and acceptance while fighting injustice and discrimination.

Mama and Papa loved their children so much and gave me beautiful memories of my youth. My grandparents were loving and comforting. Steffa, Romek and Celinka were blessings of my early years. We called my grandmother Babcia, and I can still smell her special dish of fried slices of potatoes with onions. Before the nightmares began, my happiness knew no boundaries. Afterward, when we left behind the horrible murder of our families and came to America, my dear Kopel gave me a wonderful life. I was four months pregnant and thrilled to start a new family in a new country. This was a rebirth for us. Today, my two children are my joy, and my grandchildren and great grandchildren give me nothing but smiles.

In addition to my family, I am thankful to the people who helped me write my story: Robert Arndt, Lynn Bliss, Yardena Bobys, Liz Moreno, Nadine Payn, Kamy Schiffman, and Russell Weil.

My wish for the reader is that you enjoy life and hug your loved ones, strive for acceptance and peace in this world, and be vigilant against hatred and intolerance.

—Helen Colin

CHAPTER ONE: MY FAMILY

Before the ghettos and the camps, our life in Tuszyn, in central Poland, was idyllic. Our parents surrounded us with love and made our lives meaningful and pleasurable. My immediate family consisted of my beloved Papa and Mama and their four children. Steffa was three and a half years older than me. I was the next child. Romek, my younger brother, was two years younger, and Celine, who we called Celinka, was seven years younger than me. I was lucky to have both sets of grandparents for part of my

.

childhood, and we also had a large extended family, with many aunts, uncles and cousins.

My father was a gentle man, highly respected in our community. As the owner of the village electric company, he was well known. People trusted him to arbitrate disputes that arose between families or businesses; our home was a neutral location for the two sides to come together. Papa "held court" in the dispute. First, one side presented its case, and then the other. Sometimes there were disagreements, but Papa brought the conversation under control. After hearing both sides, he considered all the information and arrived at a decision that satisfied both sides. When both groups agreed and shook hands, Mama set out tea and pastries, and everyone felt that justice had been done.

Mama was a "school mom," continually involved in our school activities; she loved to help at our school in any way she could. She was free to spend as much time there as she pleased because our housekeeper did the cooking and cleaning. Mama frequently worked in the school library and also enjoyed sewing costumes for upcoming plays. Sometimes she even served as a substitute teacher because she was at the school so often. Since all four of us children were in school, Mama could check on us throughout the day. I frequently saw her in the hallway. We blew kisses to each other, which is not to say that she did not remind us to behave and be quiet. She focused on making sure her children had the best education possible.

My older sister Steffa was like our father because she wanted to be a leader. She led us in games we played. We looked up to her, for she was one of those people who seemed to be always right. I received the clothes she outgrew and I proudly told everyone, "My sister gave this to me."

I was a happy youngster with a round face. Everyone called me "Little Moonface Child." Many times when I was scolded for a misdeed, I sulked because I was in trouble. It never took me long, however, to realize that I deserved the punishment I received. I apologized to my parents, knowing their love for me was stronger than my punishment. I always received hugs and kisses from them. Mama taught us that it cost nothing to be nice, and I still believe this philosophy.

Romek was the only boy in the family, so he was everyone's pet. He had dark hair and big brown eyes that drew people's attention to him. He was a kind and sweet child, with so much joy in him; he was always smiling. He was very friendly, and everyone in the neighborhood thought the world of him. He liked to visit people in our town, and they often gave him candy, cake or cookies. Mama scolded him for taking the food, but she always yielded to his sweet disposition. Sometimes he said that he was not hungry for dinner, and would explain, "Miss So-and-So gave me two cookies" or "Someone gave me some chocolate."

After my father died in the ghetto, Romek became the head of our family. He shared the little food we had among us, but he always gave a bit more to Mama, without her knowledge. He was like a young man with an older head on his shoulders.

Our baby sister, Celine, was an unexpected baby, but the best gift we could have had. If she cried, we listened. If she wanted a song, we sang and danced. If Celinka wanted something, she got it.

For Steffa, Romek and me, Celine was a precious toy. Our world revolved around her. Nothing was too good for our little Princess Celinka. She became a talented billiards player, able to beat anyone, often putting experienced players to shame with her abilities. At first, she was scarcely tall enough to reach the top of the table, where she could barely see the pockets, and she never missed them. When she grew taller, it was harder for her to see the pockets because she was no longer at eye level with the table. Even when she became taller, she continued to win. She would laugh and say, "Now I am going to get a cookie, because I won."

My grandparents were very close to us. My Papa's parents died shortly before the war and so did my Mama's father. Our maternal grandmother, Babcia, lived with us after his death. I am not sure how old Babcia was; to me, she looked close to 100. She had arthritis and walked slowly, with a cane. She enjoyed making everyone laugh, and her eyes sparkled with glee when she helped entertain all her grandchildren.

Once a year, usually in late August or early September, we went to Carlsbad, Germany, a natural hotsprings resort, to ease Babcia's arthritis. Babcia always returned feeling better, at least for a short time.

I had many aunts and uncles. Mama's brother married our father's sister, so we were doubly related to our cousins. Mama had three sisters and two brothers. There were six children in my father's family—including his oldest sister, who won the "Miss Poland" title. We were often with our aunts, uncles and cousins. There were many family events, such as engagements, weddings or bar mitzvahs. It was never quiet in our family!

Another person important to our lives was our housekeeper and cook, Mary. Babcia had sent Mary to work for Mama and Papa when they got married, because she did not think Mama could handle the challenge. Mary had an infectious laugh and made us all feel as loved as if we were her own children.

This Gentile woman cooked like the head chef at a five-star restaurant. Mama admonished her not to spoil us with sweets and treats. However, when Mama was out of sight, the sweets flowed.

In our small village, our family was liked and respected by both Christians and Jews. We were invited to special events, including baptisms, weddings, and first communions. We grew up involved in many Catholic events, which did not distract us from Jewish traditions. Although we did not attend Shabbat services regularly, we respected and cherished our heritage. We always lit candles and shared a Shabbat meal on Friday nights. We looked forward to Hanukah; for each day, we received a small gift as a symbol of the eight days of the holiday. We also celebrated Passover and the Jewish New Year, Rosh Hashanah.

Despite the love we had, and the wonderful times, we sometimes heard Mama and Papa whispering in their bedroom. We did not know what they were talking about, and if they realized we were within listening, the conversation ceased. At times when there were meetings at Babcia's house with members of the family, the children were sent outdoors to play. We never knew what was discussed. We did not pay attention to grown-ups' worries.

We were blessed with loving and generous parents who provided us a wonderful childhood. There was always love and laughter. How could we know that our heaven on earth would soon become hell?

Image 1: Sketch of Helen's mother as described from her
memory and drawn by Ms. Lois Gipson

Image 2: Sketch of Helen's father as described from her
memory and draw by Ms. Lois Gipson

CHAPTER TWO: CHILDHOOD MEMORIES

Things that I remember from my childhood are real to me even today. Every season had special memories, before the shadow of the war fell upon us.

When the school term was over, we spent summer at one of the villas that my father constructed. The villa had two floors. Our parents' bedroom was downstairs. Upstairs there were four bedrooms, a playroom, a large kitchen, living room, and dining room. Papa included a covered balcony around the second floor, and Mama found a seamstress to sew drapes for all the windows. We loved the balcony because we could sneak into each other's bedrooms to visit.

Papa hired a man to watch over our villa during the rest of the year, when we were not there. He cleaned the grounds and took care of the house. In winter, he cut blocks of ice from the lake. Trenches were dug deep into the ground and insulated with sawdust. The ice lasted until we returned in the summer, and we drank ice-cold beverages and cranked homemade ice cream on hot summer days.

On weekends, Papa took us on rides with the horse and carriage. (There were no cars for civilians; only the military and the city had cars.) Mama prepared picnic baskets. Papa often took us far out of the city, maybe twenty or thirty miles, where the smell of the forest air was rich with wild flowers. We thought we had left the country altogether!

When the cold winds blew in late September and the snow accumulated in drifts up to our knees and in white blankets over every treetop and roof, Papa went to the barn and got out the sled that he especially made for us. It must have been ten feet long. Papa climbed in first and we sat according to size, with Celine, the smallest, at the end. Papa's bulk sheltered us from the freezing wind. We sledded down the little slope near our house that we children thought the size of a great mountain. When we returned home, Mary prepared hot chocolate and refreshments for us as we took off our mittens attached to each other by string and warmed ourselves by the fireplace.

I have wonderful memories of my school days, before our routine was interrupted by war. We respected our teachers. We were always quiet, not even a whisper or the raising of an eyebrow disturbed the decorum of the classroom. If we needed to go to the bathroom, we raised our hand to be excused. We returned on tiptoe and slipped into our desk without a rustle.

We were assigned a single room for the whole year, and different teachers came to our room. Our seats were always the same; nobody sat in anyone else's seat, so we left our books at our desks. Each student had a wooden box where pens, pencils and erasers were kept. In those days, no one stole anything.

At home after school, Mary prepared snacks for us. After we ate, we completed our homework and Mama checked it to make sure we had done everything correctly for the following day.

Sometimes, Papa found small animals, like mice or baby chicks, for us to take to school for "show and tell." He made sure the animals were never harmed and that they were returned to their forest home the next day. He wanted us to grow up respecting nature and caring for both animals and people. However, if one of his children screamed over an insect, Papa would heroically squash it.

The weekends were indescribably pleasant because our grandparents came and visited, or we visited them. Every time that we visited them, they prepared what they knew we liked to eat, and gave us surprises. We loved to visit them.

Dinner time was always special. Papa made the rule that our dinner conversation was only for the family. Our talk should not be shared with anyone else, he said, because this was our private time. This rule puzzled me, because we were not speaking about anybody or saying anything about sadness or troubles. Instead, we talked about our life and how school was going. Babcia, who had dentures and could not chew hard food, would cut crusts from her bread and give them to us. We all wanted the crusts and would fight for them, so she took turns passing us the crust.

Our bedtime routine was also memorable. Babcia came to our bedside every night. She kissed us on the forehead and gave us a blessing before singing a song. The words rhymed in Yiddish, and in English they went like this:

You should be healthy and strong,

You should live in the nice part of town,

You should have a ton of money,

But don't be frugal with it!

We enjoyed playing with each other and with our friends. We could run and play anywhere in town without harm coming to us. There were no locked doors; we had all the freedom we wanted. There was no television, so we had to devise activities that would keep us occupied and happy.

One day when I was ten years old, Steffa and I and some friends went to a field near a windmill. Huge sunflowers grew there. We loved to roast sunflower seeds, so we picked the nicest sunflowers and took them home. One evening, while we were eating dinner, the man who owned the sunflower field came to our house. He said that he needed to speak to Mr. Goldstein, our father. Papa invited him in and asked him to sit with us at the table. He did not want to join us, but Papa insisted. Papa asked him if there was a problem. He said that he regretted to disturb our dinner but he wanted Papa to know that he had seen us picking his sunflowers. He hadn't said anything to us at the time because he didn't want to frighten us.

I knew that what we had done was not right and I asked myself how we could have done such a thing. I was so embarrassed, and I wondered how I was going to apologize for stealing the man's sunflowers. After he left, we were given a long lecture and punished: We would not be allowed to go on a picnic with our friends the following weekend. When I look back, I know that the man was not angry—in fact, he talked and laughed. He said that he wanted to tell my father because he respected him and thought that his children needed to be taught how to behave properly. Papa offered to pay for the flowers that we had stolen, but the man rejected the offer.

Another time, going to a forest to pick wild mushrooms, we walked on the side of the road, walking around light poles on the edge of the gravel. Steffa, our leader, told us to walk "straight, with your nose up in the air." When she turned around to make sure we were performing the way she wanted, she collided with one of the light poles. We caught her as she fell. She was angry with us for laughing at her, because her head really hurt. When she felt better, she understood why we were laughing and she laughed too.

When we played, we sometimes fought, as children typically do. Mama told us that we should not scream at each other. "If you want respect, you have to give respect." I still remember her words and repeated them to my own children when they were young.

We liked to put on performances for our parents. We had a gazebo that Papa had built in our garden, with steps and a platform. Mama made a drape for the back so it looked like a theater stage. We created singing and dancing routines for our parents. When we bowed at the end of each presentation, they clapped and made us feel that we had created a wonderful show!

One day we offered a different portrayal, a pretend wedding. My parents went to a wedding in Lódź, and we wanted to have some fun. My sister decided that we should perform a marriage ceremony for our housekeeper, Mary and our driver, Stashoo. We covered armchairs with white sheets and made a paper crown for the bride and draped her in a white sheet. We sang wedding songs and walked the bride around the table. I told them to hug each other because they had just become husband and wife. We wanted to drink wine but Mary provided juice instead. We had the most beautiful evening. When our parents returned, we told them about our performance, and we all laughed. They were happy because we had had a good time without them.

Daily life was more difficult in those days. Mama sewed and crocheted and taught us how to do the same. She even made our pillows, decorated with petit point and lace. Clothes were washed on a washboard and hung outside to dry in the sun. If the weather was bad, they were hung in the attic. Sheets and pillowcases were starched and hand pressed. Few people had store-bought items, even if they were wealthy.

Image 3: Helen's maternal grandmother's house in Tuszyn, Poland

My Babcia has a special place in my heart. I went to her when I was upset and she always comforted me. One time before she moved in with us, I went to her house crying because I had been punished for something. Babcia put me on her lap and told me to go hug my parents and tell them that I was sorry. She knew they would always forgive me. I did what she said and I was forgiven, of course.

Another time, when my parents were out, I came home from school crying because I thought I was going to fail arithmetic. Again, she sat me on her lap and asked me if I had done my best. She said that it was important for me to work as hard as I could. She also said that my parents would not be upset if I had tried my hardest. When my parents returned, she told them that I was worried and upset that I might fail arithmetic. My Mama offered to get me a tutor, but I didn't want one because I was afraid my friends might find out and think I was stupid. I begged her to wait until my report card came, and meanwhile I worked very hard to do well. In the end, I passed and did not need a tutor.

We knew we were treasured and loved by our parents. We knew that they protected us and wanted the best for us. I have no way to describe the joy that surrounded us and the security we felt.

CHAPTER THREE: STORM ON THE HORIZON

Return Home from the Villa

We were vacationing at our villa when Poland was invaded by the Nazis. We heard the fighting in the woods nearby and were frightened. Papa talked to us about the unsettling times and asked us whether he should sell our villa or if he should save it for us to live in. We agreed that he should keep it for us.

Our driver, who was not Jewish, left our family. Papa gave him the horse and buggy to take care of until he could return, because Papa knew there would be no place for them in the city. Since it was September, we needed to head home to Lódź, where we had moved about five years before the war began. We had to go back whether we had a driver or not. Mama, Papa, Steffa, Romek, Celine, Babcia and I began the two-hour walk back to the city. Missy, the brown-and-white spotted mutt we had adopted years ago when Papa found her and brought her home, ran after us. We took a route through the forest so that we would not be seen by the Nazis. However, we did not get very far when Nazi trucks barreled by and fired at the Polish troops in the forest. Missy realized we were in danger and stood in front of Babcia to protect her, but one of the bullets hit and killed her dog. We were spared, but Missy gave her life to save Babcia. Babcia was especially distraught, because it was her life that had been spared.

We wanted to honor our fallen heroine. We did not have shovels, so we dug a grave with our bare hands and buried her before we went further. We walked for hours through the woods. Eventually we got a ride for part of the way. We arrived home, terrified and physically and emotionally exhausted. This incident affected Babcia for the rest of her life: she could not get over how her precious, loving dog had sacrificed her life in order for her to live.

Before the war, when my parents first heard about Hitler, they considered immigrating to Palestine. At that time it was occupied by the British, so Papa applied for visas. We sold everything because the British demanded a great deal of money for each person. Papa sold our silverware and whatever we had that was valuable—except our summer villa. Our family wanted to keep it.

We traveled to Gdansk to board the ship for Palestine, but Steffa developed appendicitis the night before. She was hospitalized for several days, and we missed the ship's departure. Mama and Papa debated about having one of them stay with Steffa and the other going on the ship with the rest of the children. They decided that we should remain together.

So we missed the ship and lost the money that Papa had paid the British, who refused to return the money. Papa became very depressed. Mama decided it would be best to return to our summer villa. Because it was the summer, she was able to convert the front living room and dining room into a cozy "café" where we served ice cream, coffee, tea and pastries to make a bit of money. After a while, Mama persuaded Papa to assist in the work there. She felt that it would be good for him to be with people again, and, in fact, he regained his spirits.

But this period only lasted a couple of months. Because the war had begun, we could hear bombing and shooting in the surrounding woods. The Nazis bombed the little villages near us every day.

The bombs sounded like thunder. To this day, when I hear thunder, I am frightened. As we hid in our summer villa, my parents, hearing the shooting and bombing, grew frightened that we were so unprotected in the country. They decided that we would return to Lódź, though we had sold nearly everything and had barely anything left.

In Lódź we were to see firsthand the evil of Hitler and his Nazi accomplices, and would quickly have a sampling of the hatefulness of war. We feared for our lives and for the lives of our family and friends.

CHAPTER FOUR: CHAOS IN THE SCHOOLHOUSE

Shortly before the Nazis invaded Poland in 1939, I turned sixteen years old. A Nazi tank drove into the school courtyard, just outside our classroom. We heard the Nazis yelling and screaming. We began to cry and were very afraid because we did not know what was happening.

Our tall, blonde teacher put her finger to her lips for us to be quiet. Usually she was quite playful and kind, and even then she gave us a smile to calm us down. She then stared out the classroom window, her back to us, evidently fearing the emotion on her face would frighten us. Then she slowly moved toward her chair, her face pale, her lips unable to form any words.

Seeing the fear on our teacher's face increased our fear. Then the classroom door was assaulted with rifle butts and two angry, mean-looking Nazis stormed into the room carrying machine guns, knives and pistols. They were followed by a third Nazi soldier with a snarling, barking German shepherd on a leash.

We were terrified, thinking the dog would attack us. We were ordered to stand and form a line, then instructed to march into the courtyard. The Nazis ordered several strong boys to remove the books from the school library and toss them into a heap in the courtyard. We had been taught to respect books, and it was heartbreaking to see them destroyed as though they were garbage.

We were ordered to put our backpacks, satchels, and possessions in the pile, now taller than I. I was sad to lose all of my prized school belongings, especially a note from a boyfriend that I had hidden away in my backpack. He had asked me if he could walk me to and from school every day.

Even though it was late and the school day was almost over, we were not permitted to leave. Nor was anyone from outside allowed to enter the school yard. Then the books, backpacks and possessions in the pile were doused with gasoline and set afire. We cried as we watched our education ripped from us. Our hopes for the future went up in flames. We were then told to go home and never return to our school. We ran crying, afraid for our lives.

I did not understand the Nazis' hatred. We had done nothing to deserve such treatment.

CHAPTER FIVE: THE MOVE TO ŁÓDŹ GHETTO

After the nightmare at school, our lives deteriorated quickly. The Nazis did everything possible to shame us and deny our Jewish heritage. In May 1940, they posted notices throughout Łódź announcing that all Jewish residents must leave their homes and move to the ghetto within 24 hours. The ghetto was the poorest section of town. We could only take one suitcase. If we refused to relocate, we would be shot. As many as 300,000 Jews were forced from nearby towns to live in this small area where we were packed in like sardines.

Papa knew someone who lived in the ghetto with his family. He asked this man if he would let our family stay with him for a short time. Papa did not want to be assigned an apartment by the Nazis because it would have been very small, most probably a single room for all of us. This man had more room, and he agreed to let us stay with him.

Papa made light of the situation to make us feel more secure. He told us to bring our toothbrushes, toothpaste, medicines, soaps, books and clothes. We had to leave behind a lifetime of pictures, furniture and silverware that had been in our family for generations. My prior life was gone, and I felt as though a part of me had died. Papa told us it would be just for a short time, and we wanted to believe him because we always believed what he said. He had never misled us; why would he lie to us now? We walked through our home one last time, touching every object in the hope that we might someday return. Papa locked up the house and we set out on our way to life in the ghetto. We did not know what to expect, but I knew in my heart it would not be good. Our procession trudged along slowly from our house to the ghetto, carrying the few belongings we chose to take with us, going from a beautiful home, wrapped in generations of love and memories, to a crowded, dirty slum.

In the ghetto apartment, there were the seven of us, plus the four people who already lived there: an older man, his wife, a married daughter and a precious baby girl, only six or eight months old. The daughter's husband had lived with them, too, but had been captured by the Nazis. He would never return to his family.

The apartment had only one real bedroom, a living room and an eating area. Squeezed into a small area in the back was a free-standing stove, but there was no heat, electricity or running water. The rooms were so crowded that Steffa decided to sleep on the balcony rather than with the rest of us. I slept on a sofa bed and Celine slept on a pallet at the foot of our parents' bed. Romek also slept on a pallet. The other family slept in a tiny room, the size of a small closet. There were only two bathrooms on each floor in a building filled with hundreds of people.

We were surrounded by towering brick walls topped with barbed wire and broken glass that prevented us from leaving. Nazi soldiers with machine guns patrolled the streets. They enforced the senseless and degrading regulations that were imposed upon us. The Lódź ghetto was worse than a prison. We had no rights at all. We could not leave or enter without work passes. The Nazis forced people into trucks to be sent to work. If people resisted, they were shot immediately.

A group of Jewish leaders were in charge of the ghetto and distributed what food was available. Those rations slowly diminished. We stood in line for food for hours each day, but were lucky if we received a small portion for the entire family. Papa hunted for food in one section of the ghetto, while Mama searched in a different location. They spent most of their time trying to find something for us to eat. If what they found was rotten, Mama would cut off the rotten parts so we had a few extra bites. Papa brought a few carrots, beets, beans or potatoes, whatever he could find. He always gave the food to the family and never took any for himself. We had lived a life of luxury before the ghetto, but now we were starving like everyone else. Papa continued to repeat that we would only be there for a few weeks. We clung to this hope even as the weeks turned into months.

Babcia realized the seriousness of the situation as well and tried to do her part to help provide food for us. She thought the younger people needed more nourishment than she did, so she sacrificed her meals for us. One day, not too long after we moved into the ghetto, she went to get some of the food she had set aside for the rest of us. She accidentally slipped through the cellar door and broke her hip. She was in severe pain for several weeks, without any medical attention. Even though one of my uncles was a physician, there was nothing he could do. He came to our apartment with an empty medical satchel. He did not even have aspirin. He was devastated that he could not help her. Our beloved Babcia was the first to die because of our incarceration.

Steffa and I found work in a factory where we were forced to make uniforms for the Nazis. We walked there every morning. It was my job to sew buttons on the uniforms. I had never sewn before. At first I could not use a thimble, so my fingers were always bloodied.

Rigorous effort was required not to drip blood on the uniforms.

Each day we were given a specific number of uniforms to sew. If we did not meet the quota, we could not leave the factory until the assignment was completed. Needless to say, we tried our best to fulfill the quota so we would be given our small ration of food as payment.

The Jewish manager often screamed at us. "You're going to kill us all! If you drip any blood on any part of the uniforms, we will all be shot because the Nazis will think you are sabotaging the factory!"

We worked as hard and as fast as we could from morning until night. This factory was so productive that it delayed the closing of the Lódź ghetto for four years because of the many uniforms it produced.

Life in the ghetto was hard for everyone. People died from lack of food and sanitation. Many were shot by the Gestapo, the Nazi police force. Others died from typhus and tuberculosis.

Work crews came daily, pulling carts up and down the streets, picking up the latest round of casualties, but people died so fast, the carts could not keep up. Dead bodies lined the streets. When we first saw bodies in the streets, we were appalled by the inhumanity of our living conditions. But before long we became immune to the sight of corpses. We learned to walk over or around them. I would never have believed that I could walk on streets lined with dead bodies and just continue walking. I could not have imagined that I would be strong enough to step over corpses. How could I do that? But the reality of life was that I had to go to work, or I would not get my ration of food.

Nazi raids were another fact of life. They occurred once or twice a day, and we lived in fear that our apartment would be raided. The purpose of this was to transport people from the ghetto to their deaths. Some were taken into the forest and shot immediately; others were forced to dig pits in the forest and bury the dead. Yet others were sent to concentration camps. The Nazis developed quotas for death and ordered the Jewish leaders to meet them. Refusal led to reprisals and more deaths.

Anyone unlucky enough to be on the street when a raid took place was murdered immediately without even a goodbye to the family. All of this chaos became part of the rhythm of life, of survival, in the ghetto: looking for food, working in sweat shops, avoiding the raids, stepping over dead bodies and living without the bare necessities of life.

My entire extended family was eventually captured and sent away to death. Every day I missed another cousin, another friend or another family member, and I could not do anything about it. I am stronger today because I endured so much mental and physical pain.

CHAPTER SIX: A MOTHER'S TRAGIC CHOICE

Soon after we moved to the Lódź ghetto, Papa knew that our lives were at risk each time there was a raid. We often heard people screaming and crying, and knew that a raid had occurred nearby. We were constantly afraid of the possibility of a raid on our apartment. Papa wanted to protect his loved ones and those who lived with us, so he made a hiding place in the armoire in one of our rooms. He removed the slats from the back of the armoire and made an opening for us to enter and leave. In anticipation of a raid, we practiced quickly and quietly going into our hiding place.

A young mother and her baby shared our apartment. We loved the child as if she were our own. We enjoyed playing with her; it allowed us to briefly forget the misery and suffering around us. Life in the ghetto was depressing and hard, so the giggles and joy this baby brought into our hearts and home were welcome.

One day, our worst fear came to pass. We heard screaming and the heavy boots of Nazi soldiers in the hallway approaching our apartment. We quickly removed our shoes and climbed into the armoire. Our hearts beat so loudly I thought the soldiers would hear us. They destroyed our possessions, and their loud noise scared the baby. She began to cry and could not be quieted. If the child's cries caught the attention of the Nazi soldiers, we would all be shot. What could the young mother do to quiet her crying baby? Acting on her survival instincts, she took a pillow from the bed and laid it over her baby's face to muffle its cries. Soon there were no more cries.

It seemed like an eternity before the noise and destruction outside the armoire stopped, and it was safe for us to leave our hiding place. The mother held the pillow over her baby's face. Mama tried to pry the mother's hands away, but the baby was dead and had turned blue. The poor baby had been our escape from horror, and now it was gone. I prayed to God she was in a good place and not suffering anymore. We whispered among ourselves, wishing we could join the baby. Our lives had become worse than any nightmares we could dream.

The young mother became a zombie after that day. We led her to the table, fed her, dressed her, and took care of her. We kept her body alive, but her spirit died with her child.

CHAPTER SEVEN: PAPA'S DEMISE

When we lived in the Lódź ghetto, Papa spent the days on the streets begging and pleading, trying to find food for us. He had been head of our Jewish community in Tuszyn, a leader who helped people, and now he was reduced to begging. He became a skeleton, because he refused to eat so that his family would have food. There was not much food, but Papa did his best to provide what he could for us.

One day Papa did not return home. We knew he would never disobey the curfew, knowing that his family would fear he had been picked up. The next morning, when the curfew was lifted, Steffa and I told Mama we were going to find some food. In reality, we went to the morgue, a hut outside the Jewish cemetery. We knew that was the first place to search for Papa. We stared at bodies of men, women, and children stacked like cords of wood, waiting to be burned. Some had eyes open, staring into space. My sister told me to go in one direction to look for Papa while she went in the opposite direction. We looked up and down rows of bodies, trying to find our loving, gentle Papa. We hoped we were wrong, that Papa had found a safe place and now returned home. We did not want to find him in this madness of stacked human beings.

Papa had one toe that was crossed on top of the others. Before the war, we used to giggle when we saw his toes. When I found that unique foot among the corpses, I knew I had found Papa. His eyes and mouth were open, as if to say, "If I could only survive one more day!"

"I found Papa. He's over here," I called to Steffa. I could barely get the words out, choking on my tears. We stood next to his body, holding each other in disbelief.

We removed Papa from beneath a pile of the dead, moving body after body from one stack to the other. We went slowly and gently, because these were our people and we wanted to show respect to them. It took many hours before we finally held our Papa. We carried him together through the open gate in the brick walls of the cemetery. He was very heavy, but we were determined to give our father the righteous burial in a Jewish cemetery that he deserved.

We saw a man inside, working, and we asked to borrow his shovel to bury our father.

"Get away. There are many fathers, mothers, sisters and brothers in here. He is not the only one, and I can't give it to you," he said.

So Steffa and I dragged Papa's body to a far corner of the cemetery and dug a grave for him. We clawed the dirt with our bare hands to prepare a resting place for Papa's corpse. When we placed his body in the ground, his eyes and mouth were still open. We were so inexperienced that we did not know it was possible to close them. I could not bear to cover his face with dirt, so

I took off my threadbare sweater and carefully placed it over Papa's face. This was as close as we would get to having a funeral for him. There was no rabbi to say Kaddish, the Jewish prayer for the dead. Our tears fell on him, each tear a kiss goodbye.

We returned home to our Mama in the crowded apartment. No words were necessary. Mama could tell by our tear-stained faces that we had found Papa, and that he would never suffer again. Mama held all the children, and we all cried. How would we live without him?

Many years after the war, when I was almost eighty years old, we returned to the place where we buried Papa. I felt that I was back in the ghetto burying him all over again. We put a plaque on the wall near his grave with his name, the date of his birth and the date when we found him. He was forty-nine years old when he died of malnutrition and dehydration, because he always wanted to give another bite of food to his children.

Image 4: The Jewish Cemetery in Łódź, Poland

**Image 5: Helen at her Papa's grave,
with her eldest daughter Muriel**

After Papa died, thirteen-year-old Romek assumed
the role of "man of the house." He had been a sweet,
carefree child when we lived in Tuszyn, but he was no
longer full of jesting and foolishness. He became somber
and thoughtful about everything that concerned our lives.
All of us saw the change in him. Even though Papa could
not be replaced, we loved Romek and he loved us. He
became our protector and gave us hope to carry on.

CHAPTER EIGHT: DETOURED ON THE ROAD TO AUNTIE'S HOUSE

One day, after we lived in the ghetto for four years, I decided to try to visit Mama's oldest sister, who also lived in the ghetto. She was a wonderful woman who was very special to me.

She lived on the other side of the ghetto from where we lived. Walking to her house, I witnessed horrible things, corpses and beggars in the street, but I had to keep walking. I needed to cross a high bridge, made of two five-inch boards, which joined the two sides of the ghetto. Nazi officers stationed below the bridge would sometimes randomly shoot people on it for their own entertainment.

When I neared the bridge, I heard gun shots. The Nazis had shot a man, but his body did not fall from the bridge. It was stuck, hanging with one foot caught between the two boards. I was so distraught that I ran back home.

One other time I tried to visit my Aunt. I didn't get far down the road before sirens went off, signaling another raid. I was confused about where I was. I needed a hiding place as fast as possible, so I ran into the first vacant building I found, across the street from the ghetto hospital.

After entering the building, I heard the sound of big boots following me. There was more than one Nazi soldier trying to capture me. I climbed four flights of stairs as fast as I could, adrenaline pushing me on so I could stay ahead of those horrid boots. Finally, the soldiers gave up their chase. I heard them say in German, "Forget this lousy Jew."

I stayed in the attic of the building for a long time, afraid to leave in case the Nazis returned. The dust was so thick I wanted to sneeze, but if I did, I might have been discovered. My sneeze would have ended my life. I crawled under a dusty straw mattress on the floor. Before long, I felt like I was being smothered, so I snuck out from my hiding place and peeked out an arched window of the attic.

A huge commotion was taking place at the ghetto hospital. I did not understand what was happening, but I heard shouting and screaming. What I saw turned into a nightmare I will never forget. In a hospital window, I saw a mother holding her newborn baby, with a Nazi soldier at her side standing in a threatening position. He pushed the mother and her baby out the window into the back of an open truck filled with dying babies. Another soldier was struggling with another woman, who was also holding her baby. He grabbed the baby and threw it out the window.

My trip to my aunt's house was forgotten. Not wanting to face reality, I raced home. As soon as I opened the front door, Mama read my face. Shaking and crying, I told her what had taken place. She tried to dismiss it as a bad dream. She hugged me and held me close, trying to persuade me that my imagination was running wild. She knew I was really telling the truth, but she wanted to keep the rest of the children from panicking as well.

There may have been German people who could not do anything about what they saw. If they had helped us, they would have been shot and killed. But why didn't they stand up to Hitler in the beginning? I do not know the answer to this question.

CHAPTER NINE: "HELEN'S SICK. PLEASE HELP!"

Life continued slowly in the ghetto, but my health deteriorated. I had been a robust, healthy 16-year-old who enjoyed all that life had to offer, but the ghetto took its toll. Color vanished from my cheeks. Pain, misery and heartache took over my body. Two years of malnutrition and harsh living conditions induced severe coughing spasms. I coughed up blood and thick phlegm. I hallucinated, dreaming the misery had never happened, and we were home and peaceful again. I developed pneumonia and a very high fever.

Mama grew more worried about me every day. She did her best to help me feel better, but we had no medicine, nor even a thermometer to check my temperature. After weeks of this, she took me to see my uncle, a doctor. Even though I was eighteen, she held my hand like I was a little child. My uncle had been a prominent physician before the war. In the ghetto, he lived in a very dark room. His wife and young child had been captured in a raid and had been killed. He was devastated, but in spite of his own grief, he helped as best as he could with his limited resources.

"Helen is sick," Mama pleaded with him. She repeated emphatically, "Helen is sick, please help her!" My uncle listened to me cough and watched my suffering. He reached inside his medicine bag and showed us his stethoscope, all that he had left of his medical practice. He listened to my chest, then gave us his diagnosis.

With tears in his eyes, he looked directly at me, then at Mama. "Helen is very sick. I do not have even an aspirin for the pain."

They hugged and they both cried, and we returned home. Mama hid her fear that I might die. I knew I was very sick. The unsanitary environment and crowded conditions with little food had brought on tuberculosis. My final outcome was up to God. Once more, we had nothing other than hope, and we clung to it as tightly as we could. In the end, God's mercy saved me. It was a miracle for me to survive tuberculosis.

CHAPTER TEN: A WHIRLWIND ROMANCE

A year or so after Papa's death, an old friend re-entered our lives. His name was Kopel Kolin, the brother of my sister's fiancé, David. He was a very handsome and pleasant person, about 11 years older than me.

Kopel was nearly killed the first day he arrived. The Nazi military had sent a shipment of fifty Jews to the ghetto on their way to an extermination camp. The men were frail and old before their time, nearly starved to death and weak from enforced labor. They were scheduled for overnight detainment in the ghetto and then were to be sent on for "processing," which meant either being killed or sent to a concentration camp.

The president of the ghetto was told to guard them until the next day. Meanwhile, the Nazi soldiers went to a local bar to get drunk and look for Jewish women who they could rape and murder. They also stole from the empty Jewish homes in town and burned what they did not want, including family photos. That is why I do not have a single photo of my loved ones today.

The Nazi plan was to return the next day for their prisoners and take them to extermination camps. Kopel was one of the fifty men. He spoke to the president of the ghetto, Mr. Rumkowski, without the others hearing their conversation. Mr. Rumkowski did not recognize him at first because he was so thin and emaciated, but Kopel jogged his memory.

"Don't you know me?" he asked. "I am your best friend's son, Kopel Kolin!" The president did not react, but Kopel noticed a tear fall from his eye. In Kopel's first reprieve from death, the president arranged for another man to take his place. So Kopel was spared, but felt pity and guilt for the poor soul sent in his stead.

Kopel remained in the ghetto and was forced to work. He was a good worker, but so weak that after a while he was unable to work anymore. The president arranged for him to stay in a special house in the ghetto for a week, where he received three meals a day, a private room and a shower.

The Nazis were unaware of this place, because it was small and hidden, but sick and weak people could stay there, and the president found rations for them. At about that same time, I was awarded a week's vacation in the same location also, in recognition of my hard work. There, Kopel and I found each other. We shared information about our families. We enjoyed visiting with each other, sitting on the benches in the beautiful gardens.

It was not too long before our friendship developed into a romance. In a few weeks' time, Kopel asked me for my hand in marriage, and asked Mama for permission to marry me. I was barely 18 and Kopel was 29.

I asked Mama, "What should I do? He is old! How can I get married with all the trouble we are having?" I liked Kopel, but I was not sure about being his wife. I had never dated before the war started.

Mama helped me decide. "Helen, you deserve happiness. Our life is hard and uncertain, but it is easier when you have someone special to share the burden. Besides, if you marry him, you will get a few extra food rations and that will help all of us." She made it sound as though our marriage was the practical thing to do. So we made wedding plans.

The impersonal ceremony took place early in 1944 and was conducted by the president of the ghetto. About one hundred couples were married at the same time! It was not a traditional Jewish ceremony: there was no *chupa,* the special canopy held above a Jewish bride and groom during the ceremony. There was no traditional breaking of the wine glass afterward to indicate that a marriage had taken place. We recited our vows and were blessed by the president. Each couple received a small supply of potatoes, a carrot, a few beets and a little bag of flour, if we were lucky. Those were gifts that we would never forget. After the war, many years later, I obtained a copy of my marriage certificate, which the Lódź Bureau of Vital Records had preserved.

For our wedding reception, Mama made a feast out of famine. She took the few rations we had and turned them into a show for the guests. She put flowers on the table. In spite of the horrible location, it was beautiful. The guests were the remainder of Kopel's family and my family. I will never forget how Mama took what really amounted to nothing and made it so special to help us celebrate the beginning of our union.

On the first night of my marriage, I ran home because my new husband touched me below the waist. Mama had always told me never to allow anybody to touch me there, but now she told me that Kopel was a good man and my husband, and that this is a way the husband and wife show their love for one another.

Kopel found us an apartment near my family. It was very small, with tiny windows. He realized, like my Papa, that we needed a hiding place to use when raids occurred, and figured out exactly what to do. He moved a small table and a carpet to cover a trap door to the basement, and devised a way for us to close the trap door behind us when we needed to hide from the Nazis. He even made a pull-string to put the rug back in place after we had left the room.

After seven weeks, we heard the Nazi boots coming to our apartment for a raid. We escaped into our hiding place in the basement. On this and many other occasions, Kopel's resourcefulness saved our lives. Later in our married life, there was an opportunity for some people to leave the ghetto on a special transport. The Nazis said that they were relocating the doctors, lawyers, teachers and educated people to places where their skills could be better used. Kopel had the educational qualifications to leave with this group, and his family was going, but now that we were married, he felt his place was with me.

He did not know, at the time he made his decision, that his dedication to me and his commitment to our marriage spared his life. The "special transport" of educated men, with their wives and children, left by truck from the ghetto. Once they reached an abandoned area in the woods, they were forced to dig a mass grave. Then they were ordered to line up along the edge of the pit and shot in the head.

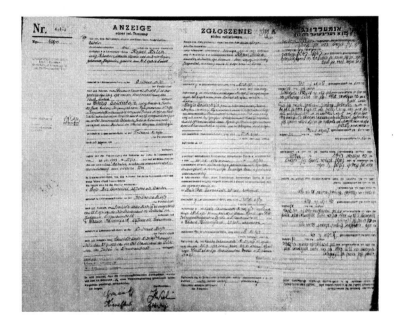

Image 6: Helen and Kopel's marriage certificate, written in German, Polish and Yiddish and signed by camp officials and rabbi

CHAPTER ELEVEN: THE LAST ŁÓDŹ ROUNDUP

Our misery in the ghetto came to an end in late August, 1944. We had lived there four years. We had no idea what would happen to us. It was extremely cold, and we had little warm clothing.

Signs about the liquidation of the ghetto were posted on bulletin boards throughout the area. If people did not leave willingly, they would be sought out and shot. Our family clung to each other, fearing the hell we were certain awaited us. We surrendered all hope as we prepared for the move, knowing there was no way to avoid the final liquidation. I mourned leaving Papa alone in his shallow grave. We had lost not only him, but Babcia, the woman who smothered her baby, the baby, her husband and countless other family members and friends. They had died of disease, starvation or dehydration.

When the day arrived, we took the few clothes that we had and we left. We no longer owned toothbrushes, toothpaste, sheets or towels. In the ghetto, we learned to brush our teeth with salt, using the tips of our fingers for the brush. We learned to live without bath soap, too. Lice and typhus were rampant throughout the ghetto. I can still smell the rotting stench of dead people in the street.

Before we entered the Łódź ghetto, Mama took gold coins and sewed them into the hems of our coats so we would have money for an emergency. By the time we left the ghetto, the money was spent. The only valuable thing we had left was Mama's gold wedding ring.

We were shuffled onto railroad cattle cars, imprisoned for two days and nights without food, water or a place to go to the bathroom. We were squeezed in like sardines, young, old and even babies, as many as 150 of us in a single car. We were packed so tightly that we could not sit. Space only became available when people died; the weak and the old did not last long. They succumbed to the foul air and the lack of nourishment.

When a death occurred, we lifted the dead person's body above our heads and moved it to a corner of the train car. The pile of bodies grew higher and higher. When the dead were piled in the corner, we created a unique seating arrangement: someone sat on the floor with his or her legs open in a V shape, then another person sat between the first person's legs and another person between his, and so on. It was the only way we could achieve any sort of comfort.

The Nazis provided us with a small enamel pot to use as our restroom in a corner of the car. It did no good because we were too crowded to get there. If we needed to relieve ourselves, we were forced to go where we were standing. People vomited from the noxious smells. This latest atrocity stripped us of what little dignity we had left.

We traveled this way for what seemed like an eternity. The stench, in the heat of the train, was unbearable. Deaths in the ghetto seemed merciful compared to the suffering we endured on the train.

After two days and two nights, we arrived at an unknown location with endless barracks stretching as far as one could see. The area was surrounded with barbed wire and barking dogs.

This was Auschwitz.

CHAPTER TWELVE: MAMA'S LAST GOODBYE

As soon as we stepped down from the train and entered the camp, Nazi soldiers with their snarling German shepherds yelled directions, telling us which way to go. Men were separated from women and children as soon as we arrived. That was the last time I saw my husband until our liberation. That was also the last time I saw Romek, the brother who had replaced Papa as the head of the family. One of the soldiers, with a flick of his hand, directed some prisoners to the left and others to the right.

We were petrified when it came our turn. Mama, my sister Steffa and I were ordered to the right.

Celine was separated from us and sent to the left. She screamed out in terror, "Mommy! I'm scared! Helen and Steffa are big girls, but I'm little. Please, Mommy, come with me!"

Mama was certain that Steffa and I could take care of ourselves; her concern was for her youngest daughter. She had to make a life-changing choice: either go with Steffa and me to the work crews, or go God knows where with Celine. She chose to go with Celine. But she could think of only one way to go with Celine. With all the courage she could muster, she removed her golden wedding band from her hand and held it out to one of the guards. She pleaded with him to take the ring and let her go with Celine. The guard did not hesitate. He grabbed the ring from her hand and pushed her toward Celine with a laugh.

Mama turned and threw us a kiss. She went to the left with Celine and other young children and those unable to work. She did not realize her choice would lead to the gas chamber. I still see her waving at us, bravely smiling and telling us to be good girls and take care of each other. We never saw our Mama or sister again.

Still numb as I saw our mother and little sister pushed away from us and after losing sight of my husband and brother, Romek, with the separation of men and women, my sister and I clung to each other as we and hundreds of other women and girls were herded, threatened and even beaten to push us toward yet another line.

We were eventually told that we were going to get showers. Always in front of male soldiers with rifles in their hands, we were ordered to strip completely naked, including our shoes and socks, and fold our clothes neatly and place them with our shoes on the ground. I felt shame. I was on a young girl.

But the shame was soon overshadowed even more by the terror and grief I felt. Steffa and I and all the women around us did as we were told. We were shoved and packed into a huge, empty room and then water was turned on from the ceiling, shocking us with cold but only for a short time. The water stopped and an exit door was opened from the outside. It was September, very cold, and we stood shivering and unable to even attempt to dry ourselves. The clothes we had left were gone. More male soldiers yelled at us to move quickly. I was freezing, ashamed and naked.

We were next ordered to spread out our arms and legs and open our mouths so they could search us for anything of value. We were then pushed along as we stood—naked, freezing, frightened and confused—to the next point were a man looked closely into our mouths. If any teeth with gold were found, he would brutally jam a pair of pliers in our mouth and pry out the tooth. Some women cried out but others just managed a whimper, their face filling with blood dripping onto their wet, still-naked bodies. The teeth was thrown into a barrel that filled quickly.

Still not finished with us, the soldiers then shoved us towards a man who pushed our heads down over another barrel and began to chop off our hair with scissors and clippers. He did this quickly and you could often see where the scalp had been gouged with the force of the scissors. Our hair fell into barrels and, once again, still naked and now bald and some of us covered with blood, we moved to the next stop.

Here, a large bucket containing a dark brown, chemical-smelling liquid was on the ground at our feet. Men passed by us with ordinary kitchen mops. They wet their mops in the bucket and threw the heads of their mops onto our heads, forcing the terrible-smelling liquid to cover our heads. As it poured over us and dripped into our eyes, it stung us horribly and continued to burn our eyes and our lungs for hours.

Finally, after all of this humiliation, pain, and physical and emotional insult, we were allowed to take a thin, worn-out piece of clothing—more like a rag than a dress—and put it on. None of the clothes fit us but we wanted anything to be able to cover up our shame and give us a little bit of warmth. We were also each given a pair of crudely-finished wooden shoes, which did not fit either. No socks. No underwear. Later, as we tried to walk in the wooden shoes, especially after it began to snow, we found out that they were extremely dangerous. The snow formed hard balls around the shoes. In a

moment, we could slip, fall and break our leg or arm.
And that would be the end of us.

Standing in the thin dress and wooden shoes that
day, I was unable to recognize Steffa or she to recognize
me. We found each other by our voices. We huddled
together, freezing, shivering and afraid, and all the women
were made to go to an open field outside. We tried to
rest and to provide each other with a little warmth and
shelter from the wind and cold.

The next day as the sun came up, we were roused out
of our quiet by loudspeakers, snarling dogs, screaming
soldiers and whistles. We were then loaded into trucks to
be taken only God knew where. My sister and I managed
to remain together. We swore to each other that, no
matter what, we would not allow them to separate us.

This was my last day in Auswitz. But, although I
didn't know it then, there were still eight horrible months
of even more hell to endure in other concentration
camps. Eight months of being nearly dead before I
would ultimately be liberated.

Romek, my brother, was just thirteen years old on

the day Steffa and I were sent to Auswitz. He was short and looked younger for his age. My husband had told me that he would protect him when we were separated.

When they arrived at the concentration camp, Kopel and Romek were initially ordered to stand in the line designated for men. Then a Nazi soldier ordered Romek into a different line for young children; they would be sent to the gas chamber.

Kopel wanted to protect Romek as he had promised. He found a large rock and quietly gestured Romek to stand on the rock next to him so that he would appear taller and older, thus saving his life.

The Nazi soldier who ordered Romek to stand in the other line discovered that he had moved to Kopel's line. He took Romek away from Kopel and hit Romek over and over again with the butt of his rifle. Romek's head split open. He fell to the ground and did not move.

A Nazi soldier said, "Take that garbage away."

That was the last time that Kopel saw Romek. He did not tell me this story until we were in America, seeking our lost relatives. He did not want to cause me more pain, but he finally had to tell me.

CHAPTER THIRTEEN: LIFE IN THE CAMPS

Steffa and I were in Auschwitz less than 24 hours before we were sent to another camp to be laborers. I did not know where Kopel was. Steffa did not know where her fiancé, Kopel's brother, was, or even if he was still alive. He had been taken away before we even settled in the ghetto. Steffa and I had only each other; we made looking out for each other our main goal in life. Over the next ten months, we worked in awful conditions in different camps, the last one in Bergen-Belsen. Had we stayed in

Auschwitz, we would have been gassed or shot immediately, for Auschwitz was a factory with no other purpose than killing innocent people.

The Nazis were in such a hurry to "process" us in Auschwitz that we were not given tattooed numbers on our arms. Instead, we received metal dog tags with an identification number. My number was 1920; Steffa's was 1921. The Nazis ordered us to take off our clothes, fold them and set them on the ground outside the showers. We were told that we would get them back when we came out of the showers; but we did not get them. When they cut our hair, we had to lean over a barrel so our hair would fall into it, adding to a large collection of other people's hair. We looked like little old men, so changed that we recognized each other only by our voices. We were then doused with some sort of liquid that burned our lungs, eyes and skin, perhaps a preventative against the typhus that was spreading through the camps. We stood naked before the soldiers and were told to spread our arms and legs, so the Nazis could check us to see if we were hiding anything.

We were outfitted with worn, torn, stained and faded dresses. I was perhaps a size six at that time, but the striped dress I was given swallowed me like a huge potato sack. Those horrid garments were the only clothing we received. We did not have underwear, lingerie, socks, a nightgown or work clothes. Wooden clogs were provided for our feet.

Rather than put us in the barracks, they took our shipment of people and marched us into an open field, where we were expected to sleep on the snow-dotted ground. We were still practically naked, because our clothing was threadbare. We blew hot breath on our hands and snuggled as closely as we could to give each other body warmth, but our feeble efforts paid us little reward. When we woke up every morning, we pinched our cheeks so we would look healthy enough to be selected for work duty each day. The only way we could survive was to be out in the yard for roll call and report for whatever duty they had for us. It did no good to complain, because complainers were killed earlier than the ones who did not whimper or whine.

One of our jobs was to carry water that bricklayers would mix with cement to make mortar. We carried large buckets, balancing them at each end of a stick laid across our shoulders like yokes on oxen in the fields. We also carried cement; it was even heavier. This was painfully hard labor, lasting from early morning till sunset. We frequently endured a day's work without a drink of water. If we stopped to rest, we would be shot.

On some days, we were sent to work in the fields. I remember being bombed by the planes of the Allies as they flew over us. The German soldiers who guarded us would hide in shelters when the bombs fell, but we were left out in the open fields. We could only crouch in a ditch or lie on our stomachs. Once, a bomb fell so close that we were covered with searing hot mud that burned our flesh. As soon as the bombers left, the German soldiers ordered us back to work.

On one of our work details I was assigned to be a welder, but I had not the slightest idea how to work the machine. Foolishly, I asked one of the guards to teach me. That was a *big* mistake! I had broken the rule that we were not supposed to speak to the Germans and I was punished on the spot. Without a second thought, the soldier took the butt of his rifle and smashed me in the face. I felt as though a bomb had gone off inside my head. Blood streamed down my face and dress. There was no way to wash it away. Because of my "insubordination," I lost four teeth. I taught myself to weld.

Other times, our group of fifty women was assigned to demolish bombed-out buildings, sometimes houses, other times deserted factories. Since we were young women, between 18 and 22, we did not know the right way to tackle the task. One day when we were tearing down the shell of a house, a huge ceiling beam hit my tail bone. The pain was excruciating! It stung like a million needles all shooting me in the same place. I could hardly stand.

Steffa and the other girls realized the extent of my injury but they refused to let me give in to my pain. I wanted to stop working immediately, but if I did not continue, the whole group would be killed. If 50 people went out to work, then 50 people had to return—a smaller number cost the lives of all. They told me that I had to return with them, whether I wanted to or not. In spite of my pain, I managed to be the fiftieth person to join the transport back to the camp that evening.

We had other jobs, such as cleaning recycled bricks, laying railroad tracks for the trains, or picking up the dead bodies around the camp and carrying them to one of the mass graves. I do not know how I carried on. I looked and felt like a walking corpse.

The guards, who felt sorry for the dogs that were placed close to a nearby fence, would take a dead body and throw it to the canines for them to eat.

A Nazi Luftwaffe base was located next to our camp. German shepherds patrolled its fenced perimeter. Steffa and I peeked through the cracks in the fence. We smelled and saw the leftover human food sometimes given to the dogs. One night we went to the fence. I coaxed the dogs to the end of the fence, away from the food, while Steffa dug under the fence and retrieved the food. There were bones with meat still on them, cabbage and sometimes potatoes. We ate this leftover mixture and enjoyed it. I would never have believed that I would be forced to steal food from dogs to stay alive, but we repeated this activity several times with a few of our friends. If you did not help yourself, you might die.

We were weak because of our previous living conditions, and life in the camp was harder than we could ever have imagined. The "food" they gave us consisted of watery soup and stale bread. What seemed like a pebble was in the bottom of each bowl of soup. We found out later that the pebbles were pills to keep us from having our monthly menstrual periods and, hopefully, sterilize us if we lived through the war. We were so ravenous that we accepted those offerings eagerly and wished for more. We always carried our bowls with us so that, if we found something to eat, we had something to put it in.

One day, we watched captured French and Belgian soldiers marching to a work detail. One of them saw how skinny and hungry we looked. They could tell we were from a concentration camp. One soldier threw a small package of food to us. It fell right in front of me.

Some of our group ran to pick it up, but I could not because it was not mine. My sense of integrity would not allow me to pick up a package that did not belong to me. I could steal food from dogs but I could not take food that was not mine, even though I was so hungry. A Nazi soldier took the package and then beat us, as punishment for trying to retrieve it.

We learned how to behave and follow rules in the camp. If we violated a rule, we were severely punished. We learned that if we felt ill, we should not go to the clinic. The ones who went never returned: they were gassed or killed right away. We learned not to talk back to the *kapos*, the prisoners in charge of us. We also learned how to march. We had to march in step, five in a row.

Once, when they marched us from one location to another, I made the dreadful mistake of getting out of step. My punishment for this transgression was to be hit in the mouth with the end of a rifle. I lost another tooth because of that beating. What a hard way to learn a lesson!

We slept in buildings like large barns. They held only a couple of hundred people, but we were packed tight, with seven hundred or more occupants. We did not have wooden bunk beds like many other camps. We sat on the floor with our legs in a V formation, each woman leaning back against the next. The one who started the first V was usually the most comfortable, because she could rest her back against the wall.

Extremely crowded conditions caused other problems. A great discomfort was lice, sometimes as big as the nails on our pinkie fingers. The showers gave us slight relief, but since the Nazis did not provide us with soap, the lice thrived.

Living each day was a challenge and only by the grace of God and the hope we had to survive were we able to endure the horrors of our situation. Steffa's determination gave us hope; we made certain we prevailed.

Toward the end of the war, the Nazis forced us to carry dead bodies from the barracks to mass graves, large pits in the earth. We had to drag the heavy bodies and were not allowed to stop for rest. A row of soldiers followed to make sure we didn't stop. It was tiring work. One day, a young girl in front of me, 16 or 18 years old, dragged a body, but she was so tired, she stopped a moment, laying the body on the ground in front of the grave. A Nazi soldier walked up behind her, kicked her into the mass grave pit and then kicked the body in on top of her. The young girl suffocated in the pit.

CHAPTER FOURTEEN: OPA, MY GERMAN ANGEL IN DISGUISE

Day after day, week after week, the stress of arduous work from early in the morning until dark took a toll upon me as well as on the other workers. My tuberculosis recurred. Frequent coughing and fever kept me wishing I could die. Many times Steffa forced me— no, *commanded* me—to get out of the barracks and get ready to work. We both knew that if I could not work, I would not live.

Steffa: "Helen, you've got to get up!"

Me: "Steffa, I can't. I'm sick and my body is weak from coughing so much blood and from fever. Please leave me here! I don't care anymore if I die."

Steffa: "Helen, I am not leaving without you. Get out of the barracks and come work with me now. Let's go!"

Reluctantly, I forced my body to do what I thought it could not. Slowly, painfully, I prepared to face the day. Steffa pinched my checks so I would look healthy and be selected to go to a work detail with her. I do not know how I found the strength to carry on. I suppose under these conditions your brain only focuses on survival. I was a robot, unaware of anything.

And then God sent me an angel dressed in the clothes of a bricklayer. He became my *Opa,* German for "grandpa." In Bergen-Belsen, my job was to bring this man water, cement and bricks every day.

One day when I thought I could not continue a minute longer, I spoke to this gentleman in German. This was risky because the prisoners were not allowed to speak to anyone, especially a civilian and a German.

"Opa, please help me die," I begged him, coughing up blood. I was working with a high fever, barely any clothes and ill-fitting wooden clogs for shoes. "I don't want to live anymore!"

This kind German man heard my request and understood that I needed his help to live and not die. He whispered to me in German, "My child, you will *not* die." As he spoke, I had to keep working, and both of us had to look at the ground for fear of being caught talking. If we were discovered in conversation, it would have been the end of me and this kind German Christian man as well. We would have been shot immediately.

"You will not die," he said, "I will help you. You will live to have a family one day and you will see your grandchildren, also!"

While I appreciated his words of encouragement, I never believed what he said. Little did I realize how prophetic his words would be.

The next time I saw him, Opa smuggled some medicine for me. "Take a capful of this three times a day," he said. "It will help you to get better." We never looked at each other. He put the medicine under a brick not far from where we were standing. He pointed to the brick so I could find the medicine.

The other prisoners warned me not to trust this German worker, saying, "He's trying to kill you!"

I replied, "What do I have to lose? The Nazis will kill me anyway if I stay sick."

And so I placed my trust in this unlikely hero. I did a clever thing to hide the medicine. I took some of the straw we had in the barracks and braided it into a belt. My straw belt worked to hide the precious bottle of medicine close to my body, out of sight of the Nazis. The medicine was a Godsend. Slowly I regained strength; the coughing and the high fever receded.

On many occasions, when Opa showed up for his job laying bricks in the camp, he sneaked little gifts for me. One of the greatest surprises was a hardboiled egg. I had not even seen an egg in five years, not since we had been forced into the ghetto! After a while, Opa grew braver and braver with the gifts he brought for me. Eventually, he brought bread wrapped in newspaper.

"Here," he whispered. "Take this and save the paper. You can read it back in the barracks. It will tell you that the Americans are close. Don't give up, my child."

The papers renewed our hope. Even those who doubted Opa's intentions looked forward to the news he brought. Compassion and hope came in an unlikely package from a German bricklayer.

He really became my German grandpa, even after we were liberated. My family stayed in touch with him and his wife after we immigrated to America. He and his wife did not have children of their own, so my children grew up calling him "Opa" as well!

Image 7: Helen's Opa in Bremen

CHAPTER FIFTEEN: THE GIFT NOT GIVEN

Every night after supper in Bergen-Belsen, we were herded into our barracks, the huge wooden doors firmly bolted from the outside. But one night, after more than a year in the camp, something unusual happened.

Rumors spread that prisoners were going to receive an extra ration of bread that evening. How excited I was! The next day, April 15th, would be my twenty-first birthday and that morsel of bread was as close as I would get to receiving a birthday gift.

Anticipation grew as the guards made the rounds. Soon they would be at our barracks and I would have my coveted gift of bread. When would it arrive? It should be any time now, just any time. As the minutes turned to hours, my dream of a birthday gift faded as the evening gave way to the night. Then we found out that the guards had run out of the treasured rations of bread at the building just before our barracks. I was so hungry I could taste and smell that bread; now all I could do was cry for my great loss.

Steffa chided me for being so emotional. "What are you doing, crying over a piece of bread? It's going to be all right, Helen. Don't be such a baby!"

Even though I was distressed, I gave in to a restless sleep. After tossing and turning all night, my hunger woke me. I still wished that the bread had been mine. But something caught my attention even more than my hunger pains, even more than my need to celebrate my special day. All of us in the barracks could sense that something was different, but we did not know what it was. Silence filled the air outside. Unlike the days before, when noise was the order of the day, this day was filled with a quiet that we had never experienced. There were no guards bellowing orders, no dogs growling to make us obey commands, no prisoners begging for mercy and no gunshots killing innocent people. No one came to open our barracks door from the outside.

We waited for what seemed like an eternity. Steffa decided we should take the situation into our own hands. Several of us emaciated women found some wood and made a battering ram. Although we were a long way from healthy, we found enough strength to knock open the huge wooden door of the barracks. When we did, we had a shock. There were no guards around, no one to tell us what to do. Instead, we found other inmates as confused and relieved as we were. God had sent the British army to liberate us from the hands of the Nazis on April 15, 1945. This turned out to be the best birthday gift I ever received. We would live! The war was over.

And the gift I did not get, the bread? All of those who ate the extra piece of the "precious" bread, died. It had been poisoned by the Nazis, because they did not want any survivors of their mistreatment and they did not want any Jews to survive. They knew our liberation was at hand, and they did their best to wipe out as many more of us as they could.

I had avoided death by the thickness of one slice of bread. Many hundreds lost their lives the evening of April 14, 1945 at Bergen-Belsen. By the grace of God, it was the birthday gift I did not receive. I believe that I was saved for such a time as this, to bear witness and to give each of you hope as well.

CHAPTER SIXTEEN: LIBERATION

We were free, and our spirits soared. We cried for joy and for the millions of people who did not survive. Our joy knew no bounds. We kissed the hands of the British soldiers responsible for liberating us. We had expected freedom for several weeks, thanks to the newspapers that Opa had given us—we just did not know when it would come. After five years of enslavement, we were finally being treated as human beings again. It felt wonderful. I still give thanks to the young men for saving us.

As we adjusted to our freedom, the British soldiers supervised the cleaning of the camp. There were still many very ill individuals and many dead bodies, especially in the barracks. The bodies had to be removed and buried in the six or seven mass graves throughout the encampment.

Very few Germans were left in the camp: most of them had escaped when they knew they were defeated. Those who were still there were drafted to bury the dead. We cursed them. We let them know that we were Jews and would live to create a future for ourselves.

We watched their every move like hawks. When I saw them dragging those precious bodies like rag dolls, I was furious. I do not know if I was bold or crazy, but I loudly demanded that they show these humans some respect, to carry the bodies and not drag them on the ground. I screamed at one Nazi in German, "Carry that body! Do not drag him on the ground. These are my people!"

A British guard stared at him, hit him on the back and told him to do as I said. I had learned German in school, so they paid attention to me, and no one tried to quiet me. The Germans actually carried the corpses with more respect. There really was no pleasant way to care for the deceased, but the least they could do was to show respect for those lost lives.

Shortly after the British came, the German civilians who lived in the nearby village were ordered to come and see what had taken place under their noses. They came dressed as though they were going to a funeral, to witness the burial of some of the people who had died in the camp. The Germans wore their Sunday best while we wore the rags we had been issued when we first arrived in the camp. They knew what had been going on behind the nearby fences, because they could smell the burning of bodies; but they did nothing to stop the atrocities.

The British wanted someone to address the townsfolk and asked us if anyone spoke German. I volunteered immediately. I asked these citizens how they could have let this go on in their own back yard. We knew they could hear our screams. We knew they could smell the smoke from the crematoria and see the ashes floating in the sky.

**Image 8: Helen speaking after liberation. Note dead bodies
piled behind her. She wore several layers of clothing,
to take to her sister.**

We also knew that people who believed in God
would not have let something like this happen. How
could they allow this to happen to us? What happened to
dull their consciences so completely? I was not belligerent
in any way, in fact, I was very gentle with them.
"Germany is a civilized country," I said. I told them that
my Babcia came to this country for treatment of her
arthritis and was treated very well—before the war. I told
them that they would have to live with the fact they did

nothing to help us. I said that I would not be angry because such anger would kill me. Some of the people remained unmoved, but some cried.

After we were liberated, Steffa became critically ill with typhus. She was confined to the camp hospital, a safe place because the Red Cross was in charge. I was not allowed in to see her because the diseases were contagious. One night, I hid below the stairs just outside the hospital. It was very cold, but I had no choice because I wanted to be with her. At dawn, I rang the bell and asked a nurse to let me in.

When she refused, I told her that I was a nurse myself and that I wanted to help the patients. She let me in. I immediately received a series of shots that would protect me against disease. They also let me use their shower. I was given a white uniform with a hat that had a red cross on it. I also had a stethoscope and a notepad to record patients' vital signs. I went from room to room looking for my sister. Finally I found her. At first, she did not recognize me because of her high fever. I asked the nurses and doctors to help her, and they gave her a little more attention than the other patients because I admitted the truth, that I was her sister and not a nurse. They were shocked, but they let me stay because I had received the necessary vaccinations.

When Steffa regained consciousness, she asked me how come I was allowed in the hospital. I told her the story and she kiddingly called me a "liar." This was the first time we had laughed in five years. She was very happy to see me. It was my turn to take care of her, since she had looked after me for so many years. The first thing I did was get her a new set of clothes. When we were offered new dresses, we were allowed to take what we wanted. I had a dilemma, I needed clothes and so did Steffa. How could I get enough for both of us and not look greedy? I decided to layer two sets of clothes on myself. I probably looked 20 pounds heavier than I actually was.

After a few weeks of rest and healing, Steffa was ready to go with me to the local displaced persons camp. It was located in Bremen, Germany. We were still in confinement of sorts, but we were clean, healthy and free, and ready for the next phase of our re-entry into the real world. Life in the relocation camp was less stressful than the labor camp had been. We were no longer slaves to the Nazis; we were able to come and go as we pleased, without anyone giving us orders. We then moved to a small room in Bremen.

Our next goal was to be reunited with our loved ones. There was a big bulletin board outside of one of the buildings. We always checked there to see if we could obtain information about our lost family members. All the displaced persons camps provided this service, so there was a network of information throughout Europe, working to reunite families and friends.

The name of Steffa's fiancé, David, appeared on a list. He was in our camp! After he found Steffa, they were married in Bremen. I attended the wedding. They lived in their own room next to the one I shared with three other women.

Kopel was in a hospital in Dachau, on the other side of Germany. At the time, he thought that I had died. Kopel found the address where Steffa and David were staying in Bremen. He left his hospital room in his pajamas because he was not authorized to be discharged but he wanted so badly to be reunited with his brother. When he left the hospital, he asked someone for pants; the person also gave him a shirt. Though he was very sick, he traveled by bus, car and on foot for two days to get to Bremen.

**Image 9: Helen's sister, Steffa, with husband David,
and a friend**

He said to one of the women staying at our
apartment, "I am looking for my brother, David." The
woman replied, "Your wife is here, too." I was upstairs.

When I was told he was there, downstairs, my legs were so weak because of the joy I felt that I could not walk; I literally rolled down the stairs.

When I saw him, I did not recognize him. His face was so swollen that his eyes were barely open, and his legs were swollen, too. Only when we hugged was I certain that it was Kopel. Shortly afterward, he was reunited with his brother and Steffa. Then he was hospitalized in Bergen-Belsen, where Steffa had been, in order to recuperate.

Image 10: After war in Bremen -- Helen and husband Kopel

Image 11: Helen in Bremen

CHAPTER SEVENTEEN: AMERICA AND A NEW BEGINNING

Kopel and I began our new life together and made plans for our future, which looked brighter with each passing day. We spent the next few months living in a small apartment near the American embassy in Bremen. We had heard that Americans were generous, and now we found it to be true. They checked on us every day and constantly brought food. They were like mother hens with the attention they showered on us. Our dignity and faith in humanity had been restored. We were proud once again.

Image 12: Helen in Bremen, taken by her husband Kopel

In 1946, we had an unexpected surprise. I learned I was pregnant! We talked it over and agreed that we did not want our child to be born in Europe's blood-soaked land. We wanted to go to America, because we had heard that there is freedom in this wonderful country. We went to the American embassy so we could tell them of our wishes. We sat in the waiting room for hours and days until someone saw us. They were more than gracious and decided to help us make the move to America.

After several months, we received word that we would be going to America, with our first stop New York City. We felt like royalty heading to a new kingdom, with four dollars in our pocket.

Image 13: Helen (left) on the ship to America

The ship was very crowded and hot, not at all comfortable. It was a freighter that had been used to transport troops and was now transporting passengers. I was sick during the crossing, and sat on the deck sucking a lemon for most of the journey. Then, one day, we saw the Statue of Liberty. I will never forget that sight. We were ready to live in "the land of the free and the home of the brave."

Our arrival in New York City marked another milestone in our lives. A Jewish service agency sponsored us when we entered the country. Kopel remembered that he had relatives who had moved to America before the war. He thought that he could just pick up the phone book and contact his long-lost cousin, David. I chided him for his naiveté, but he did not let my doubts deter him for one minute.

He picked up the phone and made a phone call. Would you believe that on the very first try he accomplished his goal? He explained to the person he called who he was and why he had called. Imagine my surprise when that person turned out to be his cousin himself! He was a college professor; he and his wife, Julia, were childless. When Kopel told them about our past and the baby we had on the way, they accepted us as their own. At long last, we had a family again.

In addition to this couple, we met other relatives. Helena Rubenstein, the famous cosmetician, was also part of our new-found Colin family. They were exceptionally nice to us. Everybody said that Americans are goodhearted and loving people and always ready to help. I never envisioned such joy and happiness as when they met us. We were so glad we belonged to somebody and had a new family. We were so much younger than they, we were like their children. There was never a moment that I did not tell my cousins how much I appreciated their kindness and generosity. Their answer was, "What do you mean? You are family!"

This was also a new life for them. The whole family knew about us. Whenever they had a party or a get-together with faculty from the university, we were always invited. We were the talk of the evening because each guest wanted to know what had happened to us. They became very uncomfortable when we started talking about our parents and the rest of our lost family. Each person embraced us and tried to comfort us. It was a wonderful feeling but it would never replace our beloved family.

Apartments were scarce in New York because of the returning soldiers and the refugees. Our cousin, the professor, bribed the landlord of an apartment building in Brooklyn by saying that he could get his son admitted to New York University, where he worked. Our cousins helped us set up our new home, and we began our new life. Kopel worked as a furrier because that had been his family's business in Poland. He took extra jobs in the fur factory in order to supplement his earnings.

When it came time for our baby to be born, our cousins were with us as if they really were the baby's grandparents. We were so happy and extremely relieved when our first child was born healthy and completely fine. We named her Muriel, in loving memory of my mother Miriam, and Beth, in loving memory of my husband's mother, Basha. After our daughter was born, the wife, Julia, always came with me to doctor's appointments to hear what the doctor said. If the baby gained a little bit or grew a little bit, we were both so happy, and she would immediately call her husband and tell him the good news. She always found time for us.

There were many times when she told me, "I love you so much. I am so grateful that you survived."

Image 14: Helen and her eldest daughter, Muriel

When my daughter was born, I was still hurting very much from the loss of my family. My heart had a great hole where they should have been. But my daughter healed my heart. I held her on my chest and knew she was in a free country. I was able to raise my child in a country where there was no hatred and discrimination. The hole in my heart will never be closed, but she healed my heart.

Three and a half years later, we were again so thrilled when I gave birth in Brooklyn to a beautiful second daughter, again healthy in every way. They both lifted our sadness at losing our first family. I rejoiced with both my daughters and now also with my grandchildren and great-grandchildren.

Steffa and David were given the opportunity to live in Houston, Texas, where David would have a job working for a tailor. Since we did not want to be separated from our family again, Kopel and I decided to move to Houston also, in 1950. We lived in this city, raising our children and starting businesses. This is where I call home. I have even claimed six feet of earth where I will be laid, next to my husband, when my time comes.

Image 15: Helen and Kopel on front page of the Houston Chronicle on May 20, 1953, for a story about their Naturalization Ceremony as American citizens

Kopel wanted to own a jewelry shop. The first one we had was very small, and we worked long hours to make it a success. In the beginning, we did not have much money for our two daughters and ourselves. I worked hard to feed everyone, making our meager food go far. For example, I would cut two eggs into sixteen pieces and add some tomatoes, cucumbers and cottage cheese. If we had bread, it was very special, but the children always had milk. Our money was limited because we had to pay rent and wanted to buy books for the children. It was difficult, but we were proud to be alive, free and have a family. Later we were able to expand our business. We sold it when Kopel and I retired.

When my elder daughter, Muriel, was sixteen years old, she asked for a car. All her friends had cars, she said. Her request came as a shock to me, because when I grew up children did not have cars. I told my husband of her wishes. He was strongly against the idea, feeling that it would not be proper.

We were still thinking of our old fashioned life in Europe, where a child would never have a car. I told Muriel to ask her father, and he said that he would buy her a car when her mother said that she did not have time to take her where she needed to go, such as the library or to piano lessons. In those circumstances, he promised, he would get her a car. That was the end of the conversation about a car. She never asked for one again because I never refused to take her anywhere.

CHAPTER EIGHTEEN: MY SPEECHES ABOUT THE HOLOCAUST

When I came to Houston, I wanted to talk to children about the Holocaust and the lessons they needed to learn from it. I helped develop Holocaust Museum Houston, with other Holocaust survivors who lived in the city and with members of the community. I wanted to teach tolerance and to stop hatred, and to protect people from harm at all costs. I am so grateful that many people came forward to help build this great teaching museum.

The Holocaust survivors who lived in Houston met, and we organized a group. We assigned people to speak to children from different schools in the area. My speech was fifty minutes with ten minutes for questions and answers. I wanted to teach young people to enjoy and appreciate freedom, to love and respect everyone and treat them as they would want to be treated.

The most important thing that I wanted to accomplish was to enable young people to understand how fortunate they were to live in this great country. I told them that they could accomplish whatever their hearts desired as long as they were willing to work hard. If hard work succeeded for me and my late husband it would work for any American child. I believe this is true.

I also told them not to hate people and not to have hatred in their hearts. Focusing on hatred is destructive. We need to love and respect one another. That is what our wonderful country lets us do.

I told the students to always tell their parents "Good morning" or "Good afternoon." If their parents were not home, I told them to wait until they returned to tell them.

"Most of all," I said, "do not leave the house in the morning without giving your mother and father a hug and telling them that you love them. You never know whether you will see them again in the afternoon." This was true and I meant it. I wanted them to understand how precious life was.

Image 16: Helen speaking at HMH

When I speak to children, there is a separation between us. I cannot tell them how wonderful I would feel if I could hug Mama and Papa once more. I hugged and kissed my father in the grave where my sister and I buried him, and children should make sure to kiss their parents while they are still alive. They do not realize how happy their parents will be with their affection. I can help children realize that their parents want the best for them and that they should appreciate them. It makes me happy to know that I have helped children through my years of speaking about my life and experiences.

When I finished speaking, I always said, "Remember, ladies and gentlemen, that you are our future. You are holding the whole world, especially America, in your hands. When you go to school, either learn or leave and go to work if you do not want to learn anything. This is your choice." I tell myself that if there were a hundred children and I only persuaded one child to be passionate and respectful to others, I have achieved something.

I have received many letters from children telling me that they learned so much from my presentations. In the back of this book are some samples of the letters that I received. I am so happy that I was able to touch the lives of so many young people. I also told my story to docents in training at the Museum. They too were moved by my story and the lessons to be learned. I was fortunate to be able to meet so many people and to touch their lives.

Dear Ms. Collins,

You're a wonderful speaker. I enjoyed learning about the war. You really touched me by what you said. I'm really sorry that all those tradgedies occured. I feel very loving toward the human race now. After seeing how you hugged everyone and don't hate the Germans it's amazing. You were an inspiration to me. Through your story I no longer truely dislike people. I understand they just go along with it. Thanks for the inspirational speech. I cried throughout it all. I never want to lose my family. Thanks to you I love them even more realizing how horrible it would be to lose them. I wish you luck in whatever you do!

Your friend,
Chrissy
Drabek

Dear Mrs. Helen Colin,

Hearing you speak about your life and the tragedies you endured really made me think. How blessed are we, the students of Clements High School, to have the life we do. You made me step back and look at my life, why do i get upset over the little things? You are such an ispiration to me♥ you are the most beautiful woman i have ever met, inside and out. You have such joy even though you have been through so much sadness. You are not bitter or mad at the people who did horrific things to you. That is the most amazing trait to have; the ability to forgive. I aspire to be like that, like you. I don't know if you remember me, but I introduced you in the beginning and handed the flowers to you at the end. I feel so honored to have held your hand and get a kiss on the cheek from such an amazing woman♥ you are te changing. God Bless♥

'ocham cię,

Madi Vartsbrunh

May 19, 2007

Dear Mrs. ~~Patton~~ Colin,

First of all, I would like to say thank you for being so brave in talking to us about your experience during World War II. Thank you for reminding us about the importance of respect for one another and the importance of life. I admire you so much for having the courage to recall that unfortunate occurence in your life.

I thought it was very sad when you told us about you burying your dad with your own bare hands. It must have been painful and very depressing. When you told us about when you were in a concentration camp and it was your birthday and you didn't get any bread to eat, and the next day you found out that the bread was poisoned,

I found that very ironic. I guess God really does work in mysterious ways. Your stories made me want to cry because what you had to go through, all that suffering and pain, is just horrible. It is incredulous how cruel people can be. I was very touched by your words of wisdom and how we should never say we hate someone. We should always try to work things out in a calm, assertive way. Thank you, again, for speaking to us and helping us to realize the importance of being vigilant and not being prejudice. I will always remember you.

Your friend,
Monique C.

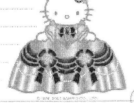

Dear Mrs. Cohn,

Your story has changed my life. I have been praying everynight for you. I am so glad I got the opportunity to meet a extraordinary woman, like yourself. Your will to live will always be remembered. When you were asked the question "Do you forgive the Nazi's for what they did?" I was completly shocked when you answered "Of course! I have no place for hate in my heart." Your words still echo in my head. My life will be forever different, for you are the person that changed it for the better. I am so thankful and glad that you came and talked to my school. Thank you so much Mrs. Cohn, for changing my life.

Sincerely,

Tanner
Holmes

Dear Helen,

Thank you so much for speaking to us on Wednesday night. Your story is so moving and inspiring. Your will to go on is truly a miracle and something all of us will never forget. I have been blessed to meet you as well as a couple other Holocaust survivors and I promise to carry on your story as well as the others. I am proud to say I am Jewish because of all the hardships our people have undergone. Just by recalling your past you change the world, and spread the word that hate cannot exist in this world. So many people do not know what the Holocaust is, and because of survivors like you, the memory will never die. As an individual, I hope to change the world, even if it means changing only a fraction of what needs improvement. You have inspired me and reminded me that any little attempt can impact people for a lifetime. I will never forget the 6 million who perished in the Holocaust. They are my blood and something I will always carry with me. G-D bless you, your family, your health, and your well-being. You are an amazing human being.

With love and Reverence,

Ben Segall

PS Attached is a reflective writing that I wrote that I want to share with you. continued on back →

I used the time given to express the pride I have in my religion and people ~~xxxxxxxx~~ as well as state my responsibility to never forget. Thank you again.

Ben Segall

I am a Jew, and I am not scared to say it. My people have been broken and exterminated but not decimated. We are still here. 6 million died because we simply are who we are. Think of all those who died: children, mothers, fathers, and the babies that never were. We still remain strong despite the fact that we as a people make up 0.25% of the entire population of the world. Imagine if those 6 million never perished, double the number to 12 million for children born to Jewish families and then add that to the 13 million Jews who live worldwide. That is 25 million Jews. The past happened though, and we can never forget. I hold pride in who I am, despite the malice my people still endure. The Jewish people have stood united for 5,000 years and will remain together through all we endure. Kol ode balevav P'nimah—"As long as the Jewish spirit is yearning deep in the heart", My people will remain strong, and filled with Hope. Never Again. Always remember the 6 million.

Dear Helen,

Thank you so much for re-living your story and all the things you fought through it really influence the way I see the world in school we learn about the holocaust and the nazi's stories, yet it never really impacted me When you started talking i was automatically moved to tears. i am a senior at Clements and i am about to turn 18. Your story made me realize that i can't complain because I have a good life i feel so lucky and now i treasure life much more. I went home last night thinking about my family. i walked in an went straight to my brother and hugged him because if we had grown up in your situation, i would have lost him. Thank you for making me a better student, sister, daughter, girlfriend, and a better person in general. You impacted me so much.

Thank you for having the courage to share your story.

Lots of Love,
Holly Chia.
Mr. Madden's 8th period Family

attached is a dragonfly i made, as these are free too.

Dearest Helen,

Words cannot express how honored I am to have been able to meet you and have pictures with you. Your story is amazing and terrifying at the same time. As I told you last night, a month ago I didn't know your name. Today, I couldn't imagine knowing the holocaust without having heard and met your story. You told us that we both even know yet how much the future depends on us. You're right. But I can also guarantee that you don't know how much our future depends on you telling us your story. It was amazing hearing you speak. I can't even imagine how hard it must be to repeat it over and over. You re-live the horror, the worst time of your life. But you also re-live the liberation on your 21st birthday. One of the best times of your life. It brings me to tears thinking how close they were to giving you that personal letter. It brings me to tears that you almost didn't get to live your life the way you were meant to. It brings me to tears knowing that I almost didn't get to hear your story. Because you changed my life, along with hundreds of others that were there. I've developed an appreciation for butterflies ♡

I promise you that for as long as I'm alive, I will pass your story on as well my children, and their children. I know you told me that Hitler is dead and you are still alive telling your story. The truth is, an evil person never lives just as a good person never dies. You'll always be alive in spirit to inspire us with your bravery. I'll make sure that it happens.

Thank you so much, and I love you too.

Linette Sanchez

2-9-12

CHAPTER NINETEEN: REFLECTIONS ON MY LIFE AND EXPERIENCES

My children gave me a new life in this country. Through children you become aware of life and how beautiful life is, and how beautiful it can be, if you just enjoy it. I always say, "Enjoy each moment because it is precious." From my past experiences, I lost many moments. I never thought that I would survive and come to a beautiful free country like America. As my children grew up, it was not always easy. I always forgave them when they did something foolish because they gave me life. I lived through them. They inspired me. They gave me the opportunity to feel happiness. I realize how blessed I was.

I feel a joy and a thrill just to speak to my great-grandchildren. It makes me feel as though I am important. I believe that I received a gift of life from God or whoever was responsible for my survival, and I have passed this gift on to my children, grandchildren and great-grandchildren.

I have one very special memory of a night in New York City when Kopel and I went to the movies. The star was Joan Fontaine, a famous actress of the 1940's and 1950's. She looked so much like my Mama that it seemed as though she had come back to life. Her emotions were just like my Mama's. I was so overwhelmed that I could not watch the rest of the movie. Years later, when the children were older, my husband told them this story. On my birthday my oldest daughter gave me a copy of Joan Fontaine's autobiography, *No Bed of Roses*. They inscribed it, *"To Mama (4/15/1979): Hope you have a wonderful year and many, many healthy, happy years to come. Love, 3 M's." (Muriel, Marcel and Michele).*

I was so happy to have a picture of Joan Fontaine, who looked so much like Mama. Even now, after all these years, I look at Joan Fontaine's picture on the book cover, and I stroke her face and whisper, "Good night, Mommy. I love you." In my spirit I feel Mama speak to me, "My darling Helen, I love you too." It's all pretend, of course; I know she is not my mother. But I do it just the same.

My daughters were American citizens before me. When my oldest daughter was born, I told my husband that we had to become citizens also. My beloved adopted America has given me opportunities that I would never have had anywhere else in the world. American citizenship gave me freedom, and an opportunity to educate my children. This was a priority for me, because I had been chased from school when I was sixteen. It gave me the opportunity to feel free to travel anywhere.

I took my children and grandchild back to the place where I was born and showed them my home and school. They were overwhelmed. The trip reminded them that their parents were also young at one time. I am blessed in so many ways. I am proud to say that I will never be evacuated from our blessed country.

Image 17: Helen with her wall of treasures

On my living room wall, I have hung wonderful pieces from my past that I look at every day. I want people to see my mother's and father's birth certificates, and my marriage certificate. They are my treasures, recovered from the ghetto after sixty-five years. There is also a sketch of Mama and Papa that was drawn in Houston by a volunteer from Holocaust Museum Houston, based on my description and the picture of Joan Fontaine. It is a close resemblance to my Mama. This is the only visual reminder that I have of her. Some photos of the pictures from the wall are located throughout this book.

It is such a joy to live in America and call it my home. I did not get a piece of the poisoned bread. I was allowed to live. And the longer I live, the more amazed I am that I still can stand on my weak feet and that my brain is still working. It is beyond comprehension how much you can do and what you can achieve here. I continue to hope for peace in the world, peace for everybody. It is such a pleasant life, when there is peace.

.

Image 18: Papa's birth certificate

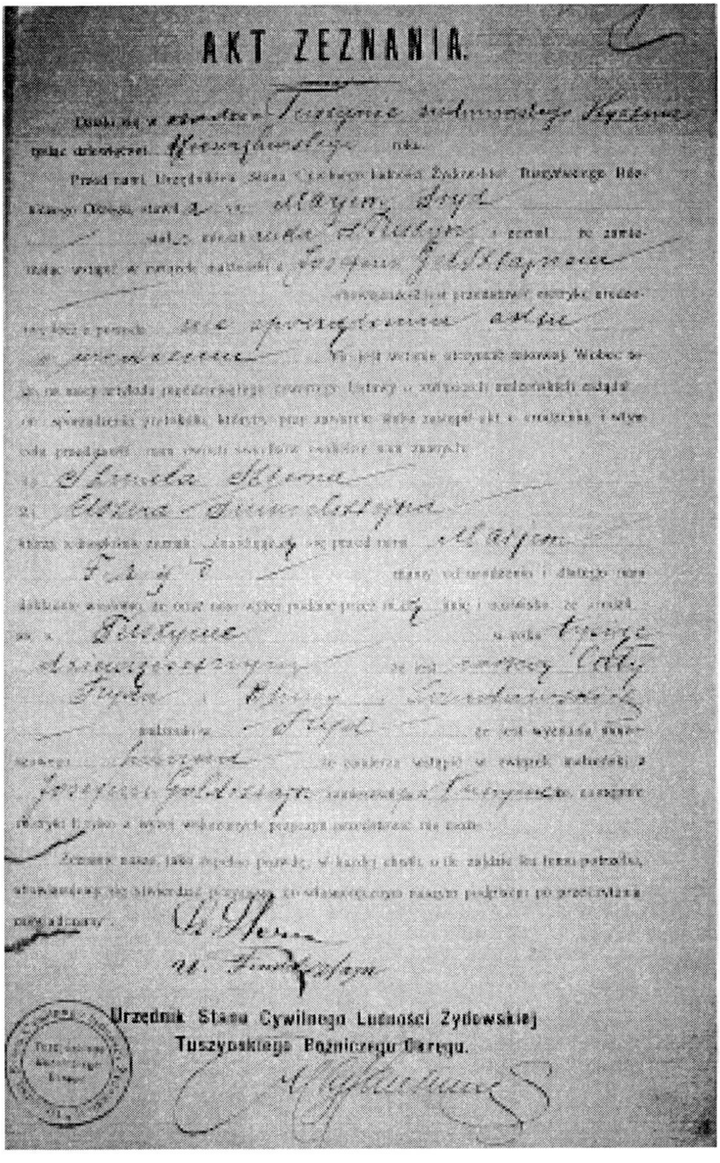

AKT ZEZNANIA.

Urzednik Stanu Cywilnego Ludnosci Zydowskiej
Tuszynskiego Pozniczego Okręgu.

Image 19: Mama's birth certificate

I love my new country. I smile whenever I see someone. I greet them and say that we are going to have a great day, even if I do not know them. It is so easy to smile. I promised myself that my smile will give people a good feeling. My grandma always said that it costs nothing to be nice. I pray that innocent people will not be murdered. I cannot understand how innocent people can be killed daily. I pray that before I go, that there will be peace in America and throughout the world.

I know that there are problems around the world, violence and wars that scare me. But we must protect and love each other. What happened to the Jews must never occur again. We must always be vigilant against such horrors.

Image 20: Helen with Ellie Wiesel

Image 21: Helen with Bob Dole

POSTSCRIPT: HOW I MET HELEN COLIN
By Elizabeth Dettling Moreno

I became interested in Holocaust studies in 1996 when I first started teaching at Bay City Junior High. *Devil's Arithmetic* was on another teacher's agenda, so I followed her lead. Up until that time, I'm not sure that I had even heard the word *Holocaust*, and I certainly did not realize what it involved. Because of that original experience, I can honestly say I'm not who I used to be. I have become passionate about teaching the lessons of the Holocaust so this generation of adolescents may bear witness to future generations.

Two years later, I insisted that my husband accompany me to the Holocaust Museum in Houston so that I could see for myself just what took place during that era. I was dumbfounded to see what great efforts the Nazis made to torture the Jews. An idea began burning inside me to bring our students for a field trip so that they, too, might gain an appreciation for this time in history. It took a bit of coaxing to get our principal to agree, but we finally succeeded in arranging a trip, and we have visited almost every year since then.

That year I heard Walter Kase's story for the first time. As a teenager, he had been a captive in the Mauthausen camp. After liberation, he relocated to the Houston area. When he finished by telling about his liberation, my heart started pounding as he talked about the American tank driver who got out of his tank, talked to him about the horrors he was seeing, and then gave him a Hershey's chocolate bar with almonds.

My dad, John Dettling of Wharton, Texas, had told us that same story as we were growing up—but in his version, he was the driver! When I was a child, it was just a story without much meaning, but now it became real! I sobbed and sobbed as I retold Dad's share of the story to Walter and the students in the room.

I ended up writing a letter to Mr. Kase and the museum describing that unique relationship. The following year, Dad received an invitation from the museum to share his war stories for the archives as one of the liberators. He went to that interview and his fascinating stories are now preserved for future generations. Then Dad and Mom were invited the following year to a special banquet to honor the liberators. I certainly wished I could attend with them, but tickets were $500 each. There was no way we could afford that amount of money, but something happened to spark an idea and make it possible.

My younger sister Helen and her husband Mark Monfrey lived in Dallas, and one of my cousins, Sister Karen Kudlac, taught in a nearby school. She invited Dad to come visit her classroom to share his war stories, so he and Mom made a trip to Dallas. Somehow her students found out about the banquet and took it upon themselves to take up a collection to make a third ticket possible. Joyfully, they handed dad $265 in cash, over half the cost of the coveted ticket.

Upon their return home to Wharton, Mom and Dad shared their wonderful news with the rest of the family. If these students we had never met could give such a nice gift to strangers, couldn't I do something as well? That was when I decided I could, and the next morning, before the sun came up, I started making Rice Krispies treats to sell for a dollar each to hungry students. I made sure that the squares were large enough to entice the students to buy, buy, buy. Within a couple of weeks—and dozens and dozens of Rice Krispies treats later—we had enough money and I was well on my way to being part of the celebration. (We were given a few donations toward our goal, too.)

The night of the banquet, we met a most remarkable lady, survivor Helen Colin, and members of her family. After the field trip with our students, her portion of the video with survivors stuck with me permanently, especially the story of her Mama's last goodbye. Because of her prominence in the video, I was hesitant to invite her to speak at our school; I thought the chances she would actually come were slim. But she graced us with her presence and did so again for many years. She has shown that it is her great delight to share her experience, and for that we are truly grateful.

Image 22: Helen with liberator John Dettling

Because of that encounter on the night of the banquet, Mrs. Colin and I forged a strong bond that goes beyond ordinary acquaintanceship. In our conversations that evening, we realized that my dad had helped to liberate Buchenwald, the camp where her husband had been confined. This made our connection even stronger, and she tearfully hugged my dad as her hero. I call her my

Jewish Mama and she tells others that I am her adopted Gentile daughter. It is my great delight to honor her by writing her memoir.

May you, the reader, be as blessed by reading this as I have been by knowing this wonderful lady.

Shalom,

Elizabeth Dettling Moreno